## Walkthrough

This book is called 'Josie and the Junk Box'.

What do you think 'junk' is?

Do you ever make things out of junk?

Remind the children of the other Josie stories they may have read.

## Walkthrough

This is the back cover – let's read the blurb together.

'What can they make?'

(Prompt for suggestions.)

## Walkthrough

This is the title page.

Read the title with the children again.

What do you think Josie and her friends might do with the junk?

What sort of junk do you think they will find?

1

What can Josie see?

How might Josie be feeling?

 **Observe and Prompt**

### Word Recognition

- Check the children can read the word 'I'. (This is a sight word – a word likely to be in their store of familiar words.)

- Check the children are reading the CVC word 'can' using their decoding skills. Can they sound out and blend c-a-n all through the word?

- The words 'wool' and 'buttons' may not be decodable for children at this stage. Tell the children these words.

2

**Observe and Prompt**

**Language Comprehension**

- Ask the children what Josie is saying.
- How do the children think Ravi is feeling?
- Check the children can identify the junk box and explain what it is.

# Walkthrough

What can Josie see now?

 **Observe and Prompt**

### Word Recognition

- If the children have difficulty with the word 'bottle', ask them if they recognise the initial letter and sound – 'b'. Then tell them the word and model the reading of this word for them.

- The word 'straws' will not be decodable for the children at this stage. Tell the children this word.

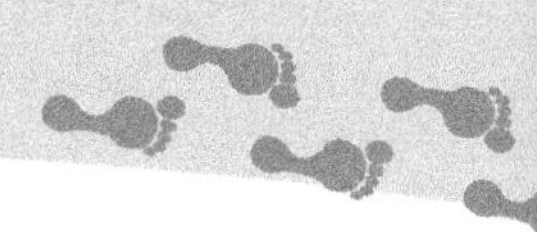

**Observe and Prompt**

**Language Comprehension**

- Ask the children what Josie's friend Tilly can see now.

- Ask the children how Josie might be feeling.

- What else do the children think might be in the junk box?

 **Observe and Prompt**

### Word Recognition

- Check the children can read the CVC word 'big' using their decoding skills.

- Check the children are reading the CVC word 'box' using their decoding skills. Can they sound out and blend b-o-x all through the word?

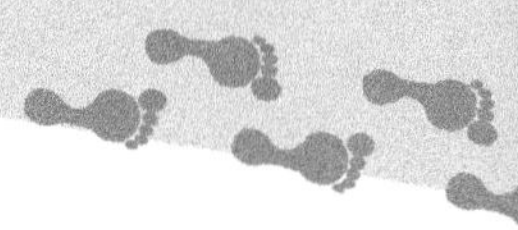

**Observe and Prompt**

**Language Comprehension**

- Ask the children what Ravi
  can see now.

- Ask the children what they
  think might happen next.

**Walkthrough**

What have they made?

Make sure the children realise this is a monster.

 **Observe and Prompt**

### Word Recognition

- Check the children can read the sight words 'we', 'see' and 'a'.

- If the children have difficulty with the word 'monster', ask them if they recognise the initial letter and sound – 'm'. Then model the reading of this word for them.

 **Observe and Prompt**

### Language Comprehension

- Check the children understand what has happened at the end of the story. What have they made?

- Ask the children what the children in the story are saying.

8